DOMIN8 YOUR DAY

Cate

student edition

30 Empowering Statements That Encourage Greatness

This book is made interactive by InterApp. Download the app and scan the book cover for exclusive content. Beginning February 18, 2019.

DOWNLOAD
INTERAPP
TO INTERACT

Domin8 Your Day: 30 Empowering Statements
That Encourage Greatness
Visit the author's website:
www.dwighttaylorsr.com

Published by E Squared Publishing Group, a
Cortney Sargent company.
E Squared Publishing Group
www.esquaredpublishing.net

Edited by Emma Barry.

DEDICATION

This book is dedicated to all of my teachers (especially Suzanne Smith and Mr. Green), coaches, counselors and mentors that treated me like a human being instead of just a student or athlete. THANK YOU! I do what I do because of YOU.

CONTENTS

INTRODUCTION

Only Phenomenal and Amazing people open this book. And, in your case, you are BOTH. That makes you PhenomenAmazing. I probably don't have to tell you that your life isn't only about existing. I probably don't even have to tell you that your life isn't only about surviving. With you being the awesome person you are, I'm quite sure that you know your life should include THRIVING! But, since you're here, let me ask you some questions:

Could you use some help overcoming procrastination? Self-doubt? Negativity? Low self-esteem? Making excuses?

Do you find yourself being unable to make wise decisions? Truly forgive? Be patient? Show empathy? Exercise leadership? Stay loyal? Follow through?

Are you unsure about how to handle discouragement? Failing? Your past? Distractions? Responsibilities? Tragedies?

If you answered YES to any of these questions, THIS BOOK IS DEFINITELY FOR YOU!

Self-awareness is the name of the game; and

the game is life-long. The sooner YOU learn YOU, the sooner you will be on your way to living a fulfilled life.

"Domin8 Your Day: 30 Empowering Statements That Encourage Greatness" is a high-energy, high-value, interactive book that will take you through insightful explorations of how self-awareness can positively impact your life and the lives of others.

Packed with empowering statements, encouraging summaries, transparent stories and transformative questions, this book will help you be the very best version of yourself that you were created to be, in every moment of your day. Now let's get to it!

How to use this book & get the most out of it:

1. **Read the main statements** – There are 30 main empowering statements.

2. **Relate the summaries & stories** – Each statement is followed by either a summary, story or both. Try to relate these to your life.

3. **Reflect on the questions** – The

summaries and statements are followed by questions for you to reflect on and then answer.

4. **Respond with action** – Go and DO!

The best way for you to navigate through this book, is the way that works best for you. I suggest that you complete a statement set (all 4 components) each day or every other day. Again, this is just my suggestion. Make this work for you! Now go and **Domin8 Your Day**.

Oh yea... feel free to contact me if you have any questions, need any help or extra encouragement along the way. *DwightTaylorSr@gmail.com*

BE YOUR BEST. FORGET THE REST. GIVE YOUR PERFECT EFFORT AND NOTHING LESS.

1

Be Your Best. Forget The Rest. Give Your Perfect Effort And Nothing Less

Every morning you wake up; do a self-assessment of the person you were the day before. Then go out and COMPETE with yesterday's you. Don't just DO more than you did yesterday...BE more than you were yesterday.

In everything you do, make sure you give your perfect effort. My brother Andre "S.O.G." Ward says, "Effort is between you and you". Listen, only YOU know how much effort you are putting into what you're doing and if you're being the very best YOU that you were created to be. It's easy to APPEAR as though you are giving 100 percent, but if you know you are only giving 70, 80, or even 90 percent, then I challenge you to evaluate the motivation behind your actions.

You may feel giving your perfect effort is risky because there is no guarantee of the outcome that you want. But, you are only robbing yourself by not giving your all. **You cannot know your full potential until you give your full effort.** Don't let a moment, second, minute, hour, day, week, month or year go by without giving your PERFECT EFFORT. Your future you will thank you for it. **#Domin8YourDay**

Q&A

What areas of your life have you given your perfect effort? Why?

In what areas of your life do you need to be better at giving your perfect effort?

How will you practice giving your perfect effort in every area of your life?

How will you benefit from this?

How will the people who care about you the most and the people you care about the most benefit from you giving your Perf3ct Effort?

2.

Every Decision Matters

Decisions matter! **Every single decision made for you and by you have landed you right where you are in life at this very moment.** If you are not excited with where you are, then challenge yourself to start making different decisions. Listen, once you start making decisions, your decisions start making you. So, right now is a **#PhenomenAmazing** time to reflect on your decision-making process. Ask yourself why you've decided on the things that have gotten you to your current point. Once you figure it out, make small adjustments and make new decisions. I encourage you to decide wisely. Your future you will thank you for it. **#Domin8YourDay**

Q &A

What are some great decisions you've made in the past week?

What about these decisions makes them great?

What's the best decision you've made today?

What can you do to push yourself to make wise decisions?

How will you benefit from this?

How will the people who care about you the most and the people you care about the most benefit from you making healthier decisions?

IF YOU START IT, FINISH IT

3

If You Start It, Finish It

If you start it, finish it. Perseverance is the key. No matter how tough it gets or discouraging it looks, refuse to give up. Stay determined. Stay dedicated. Stay hopeful. Keep your eyes on the goal. Today is YOUR day to persevere and push past those things that are holding you back from dominating your day! Before you allow yourself to quit anything, **remember why you started** in the first place. Take time to reflect on the feelings that you had when you started. Think about the people who are depending on you to not only finish, but finish strong. A sense of HIGHEST URGENCY is needed. Constantly remind yourself of the great things that will happen once you complete your task at hand. So, don't give up. Don't give in. Just give it ALL you got. Your future you will thank you for it. **#Domin8YourDay**

$$* * *$$

Q&A

What are some things that you've started, but haven't finished?

What is stopping you from finishing these things?

How can you put forth the perfect effort to finish the things that you start?

How will you benefit from this?

How will the people who care about you the most and the people you care about the most benefit from you finishing what you started?

4

Even At Your Worst, The Right Person Will Still Feel That You Are Worth It

#Transpar3ntTuesday Entry

There have been many times in my life where I tried to be "someone" else for the wrong people. But, I could only pretend for so long because it started to make me extremely unhappy. Pretending to be someone/something else is tiring, draining and plainly put...WACK! When you pretend to be someone else for another person's approval, you are saying that you aren't good enough as you are! So, **never pretend just to win** a person's approval. You are better than that. Surround yourself with people who see your worth even at your WORST and encourage you to do and be better. I'm blessed to have these type of people in my life. The dope thing is this: there will always be someone who loves you at your worst. Find peace in that.

I encourage you to remove yourself from people and situations that make you feel like you are worthless. Your future you will thank you for it. **#Domin8YourDay**

Q&A

Who stood by you during your worst?

How can you use what you've learned to see someone else's worth even at their worst?

How can you go about acknowledging your worth on a daily basis?

How will you benefit from this?

How will the people who care about you the most and the people you care about the most benefit from you removing yourself from people who won't accept you at your worst?

P L

5

Turn Your Obstacles Into Opportunities

Recently, our Einstein Middle School girls' basketball team, The Lady Eagles, were down by 9 points with under one minute left in their game. On the outside looking in, this deficit may have seemed like an unbeatable obstacle. But, our girls chose to see it as an opportunity. Instead of focusing on those 9 points as something they couldn't overcome, they looked at the seconds they had left as a chance to show their strength and resilience. By choosing to use the seconds they did have instead of dwelling on the points that they didn't have, The Lady Eagles actually ended up grabbing the "W" in overtime by two points. (*Shout out to Coach Roberson.*) When the girls chose to see past the points they didn't have (obstacle)and focused on the handful of seconds they had(opportunity), they were choosing to switch their perspective. Or, how they saw the situation. In showing their strength and resilience rather than seeing their deficit as something they couldn't overcome, they turned their obstacle into an opportunity. So, today is your day to **switch your perspective when it comes to your obstacles.** Turn each and every obstacle into an opportunity to succeed. Your future you will thank you for it. **#Domin8YourDay**

Q&A

What is an obstacle that you're facing right now?

Why is it an obstacle for you?

How can you switch your perspective and turn this obstacle into an opportunity?

How will you benefit from this?

How will the people who care about you the most and the people you care about the most benefit from you turning obstacles into opportunities?

CHARACTER IS DISPLAYED IN HOW YOU REACT

6

Character Is Displayed In How You React

Here are two words that can help you on your journey to being a great man or woman of character: **Respond Well.** Let that soak in, respond well. Those two words can keep you from assassinating the mental and moral qualities distinctive to you because they cause you to THINK before you ACT. My grandfather once said to me "talent will get you there, but it will be your character that keeps you there". **ALWAYS MAKE SURE THAT YOUR CHARACTER IS ON TEN!** Constantly remind yourself that someone is always watching you. Someone is always listening to you. Someone is always observing you. Their reasons for observing you can be positive or negative. Regardless of their reasons, just make sure to keep your character at its highest level at all times. Your future you will thank you for it.

#Domin8YourDay

* * *

Q&A

Do you practice responding well to people and/or situations?

How can you improve the way you respond to people and/or situations?

What are some ways you can continue to keep your character at it's highest?

How will you benefit from this?

How will the people who care about you the most and the people you care about the most benefit from you responding well in all situations?

7

Separation Can Lead To Elevation

Separation is a key component in the process of elevation. We must first separate from the NEGATIVES that weigh us down... negative thoughts, negative actions, negative habits and negative people. We must then separate ourselves from the mediocre in order to be good, the good in order to be great and the great in order to be EXCEPTIONAL! **It won't be easy BUT it doesn't have to be complex.**

If you are struggling with reaching your next level in life, it could have something to do with what is attached to you. That "what" could be a person, past experience, habit, way of thinking or all of the above.

For many of us, there are negative past experiences that keep us in a state of low-level living. Because of these experiences, we never truly soar with wings like eagles. And, it's not so much these past experiences, themselves, but more so the feelings that come with these experiences. If you begin to look at your past negative experiences as experiences that happened "for you" instead of happened "to you", you will put yourself in a better position to see them as learning and growth opportunities.

Maybe it's a habit that's been hindering your growth. If that's the case, then you must put a stop to that poisonous habit and start a new productive one. Identify the WHY of the poisonous habit and make small adjustments to replace it with a new and productive habit with a positive WHY.

If it's a person that's holding you down, help yourself out by having the courage to cut that person out of your life. Sometimes you have to cut ties, in order for you to rise.

If it's your way of thinking that's affecting your elevation, then renew your mind and keep positive thoughts in rotation. You can renew your mind by meditating on things that are true, noble, just, pure, and lovely. These 30 statements can assist you in keeping positive thoughts in heavy rotation. I know this may all sound basic, but these are some key ingredients to greatness. I encourage you to add these ingredients to each moment of your day. Your future you will thank you for it. **#Domin8YourDay**

***

Q&A

Who and/or what do you need to separate from in order to achieve elevation?

How will you separate?

How will you benefit from this?

How will the people who care about you the most and the people you care about the most benefit from you separating in order to elevate?

VALUE IS HIDDEN IN YOUR VALLEYS

Value Is Hidden In Your Valleys

In our life, we move through high points (mountaintops) and low points (valleys). Being on our life's mountaintops, can encourage us to feel strong, happy and even unstoppable. When we are down in our life's valleys, we can easily become discouraged. We may even feel that our situation will never change or get better. But, in the same way that you can find purpose in your pain, you can find **VALUE IN YOUR VALLEYS**. When you feel you are deep down in one of your life's valleys, I encourage you to rethink your perspective. Look for ways to learn and grow. By changing your perspective, you can open your eyes to all the value hiding in that valley. Rather than being consumed by discouraging thoughts and feelings of defeat, you can begin to see that optimism can occur in your valley. Courage can be cultivated. Appreciation can be achieved. Life lessons can be learned. And, victories can even be produced IN. YOUR. VALLEY. There may be times when you have to push yourself a little harder in order to find the value...*STAY STRONG!*

So, the next time you find yourself down in a valley, **take comfort** in knowing that through this experience you'll find the value hidden within it. Your future you will thank you for it. **#Domin8YourDay**

Q&A

Do you find yourself becoming discouraged when going through low points (valleys) in your life?

Are you currently moving through a valley in your life?

What can you do to look for the value in the valleys of your life?

How will you benefit from this?

How will the people who care about you the most and the people you care about the most benefit from you finding value in your valleys?

SHORT-TERM SACRIFICES CAN LEAD TO LONG-TERM LUXURY

9

Short-Term Sacrifices Can Lead To Long-Term Luxury

Sacrifice: An act of giving up something valued for the sake of something else regarded as more important or worthy. My wife and I recently sacrificed a trip to Las Vegas. We made this sacrifice to avoid putting ourselves in a bad financial situation. Yes, we could've easily gone to Vegas. But, we wouldn't have been able to really enjoy it because we would've been thinking about all of the financial responsibilities waiting for us when we got back. Because of our short-term sacrifice, we have the long-term luxury of planning a better trip and being able to fully enjoy our time away.

There are times when our NOW has to be sacrificed for the sake of our NEXT.

There will be times when you have to sacrifice who you are (the short-term) for who you could be (the long-term.) Maybe you have to practice harder in order to win that championship or become the best at what you do. Maybe you have to study longer to pass that test or acquire the knowledge you need to be seen as an expert. You might have to get to work earlier and stay later in order to bring home the income that will put you in a position to gain financial freedom. And, if that's what it takes for you to enjoy the rest of your life, then that's what it takes. If you and the people you care about are able to live a better life down the line because you sacrificed, then sacrifice. Give up the good things for the greater things. This can only happen if you are focused on the long game and are truly WILLING to make the sacrifice. If you are more concerned with now than later, you will not see the benefits of sacrificing your now for a greater later. So, I encourage you to think long-term while make short-term sacrifices. Your future you will thank you for it. **#Domin8YourDay**

Q&A

What are you willing to give up, in order to go up? Why?

What is the most recent short-term sacrifice you made that benefited you and others in the long-term?

What was your thought process for that sacrifice?

How can you apply that same thought process to future sacrifice?

How will you benefit from this?

How will the people who care about you the most and the people you care about the most benefit from you making a short-term sacrifice for a long-term reward?

10

Storms In Your Life Don't Come To Break You, They Come To Shape You

Your life will never be storm free. Because change is constant, something is always bound to happen. When that something does happen, don't run from it. Or simply just GO through it. I encourage you to GROW through it. Listen, **the very characteristics that you need, can only be developed as you grow through the storm.** All you need is a change of perspective. Stand firm and embrace the storm. See what you can learn about yourself as you engage the storm. Then take comfort knowing that not only will you be stronger after the storm BUT you will also be wiser. You will then be able to take that strength and wisdom to help someone else get through their storm! Your storms might bend you, but don't let them break you. In the profound words of Martin Payne, "Don't break. Don't break. Don't break." If you don't let your storm break you, you will see your breakthrough. So, stay encouraged and BELIEVE for your breakthrough. Your future you will thank you for it. #Domin8YourDay

* * *

Q&A

What type of storms are you currently facing?

How are you responding to them?

Why are you responding this way?

How can you push yourself to grow through these storms?

How will you benefit from this?

How will the people who care about you the most and the people you care about the most benefit from you embracing your storm and getting your breakthrough?

11

Initiate Change So Things Don't Remain The Same

It only takes one person to spark millions. Stop waiting for someone else to do what you desire to see be done. Don't even wait until you feel pressured to initiate change. Be the one to apply pressure to the situation. Some things in life won't change unless you change it. That's right. **IT'S ON YOU!** And, I don't want to hear you talking about *"I'm waiting on the perfect time"*. If that's the case, you will be waiting forever for change to happen.

Initiating change doesn't mean that you have to make things happen all by yourself. Just be bold enough to kick-start the change, so things don't remain the same. Your future you will thank you for it. **#Domin8YourDay**

Q&A

Do you initiate change in your life?

In what areas of your life do you need change to occur?

How are you going to make these changes happen?

How will you benefit from this?

How will the people who care about you the most and the people you care about the most benefit from you initiating change?

ACKNOWLEDGE YOUR PROGRESS IN THE MIDST OF YOUR PROCESS

12.

Acknowledge Your Progress In The Midst Of Your Process

Listen, far too often we're so concerned with perfection that we miss out on the progression. While you may not be where you want to be, you're certainly not where you used to be. Acknowledge that. Feel good about the fact that you have made it this far. **Don't allow the pursuit of perfection to overshadow your progression.** I encourage you to always acknowledge when you progress. Your future you will thank you for it. #Domin8YourDay

Q&A

What type of progress have you made in the past week? Month? Year? 5 years? 10 years?

How do you feel about each of these progressions individually?

Why do you feel this way about these progressions?

Did you acknowledge your progress in each of these moments? Why or why not?

How can you go about acknowledging your progress in the future?

How will you benefit from this?

How will the people who care about you the most and the people you care about the most benefit from you acknowledging your progress in the midst of the process?

13

Speak Life Into Someone Today

When I was twelve, Sharon Osteen was my principal. She didn't look like me or come from the same type of upbringing as me. And, on top of that, I always felt she disliked me. But, one day she changed my life. She told me that I would be a great leader someday and that I had GREATNESS inside of me. Hearing something like this straight from my principal's mouth rocked my little world. The icing on the cake was that I was crazy enough to BELIEVE what she said was TRUE. This moment always reminds me that WORDS HAVE POWER! **In your words, you have the ability to change a person's life...FOREVER.** I'm grateful to my principal for speaking these life-altering words to me. I still believe in them 24 years later.

Hear me loud and clear. YOUR WORDS HAVE POWER! Just as they can have a positive effect for years they can also have a negative effect. So, mind your words. And, I encourage you to be intentional about speaking LIFE into someone today. Your future you will thank you for it. **#Domin8YourDay**

Q&A

Has anyone ever spoken life into you?

If so, who was it?

Do you ever speak life into other people? Why?

How can you continue to challenge yourself to speak life?

How will you benefit from this?

How will the people who care about you the most and the people you care about the most benefit from you speaking life into someone today?

DON'T EXCHANGE WHAT YOU WANT MOST FOR WHAT YOU WANT NOW

14

Don't Exchange What You Want Most For What You Want Now

The other day I was talking to my younger brother. He was telling me that he wanted to buy a car in order to get from point A to point B and to his job without asking for rides. In the same breath, he told me about how he was going to go out and buy more shoes and jeans. I gently reminded him not to exchange what he wanted most (a car) for the fleeting things he wanted right now (jeans and shoes). How many of us do this? We make a goal for the future, but forget about making the small adjustments to achieve them when faced with the temporary "right now wants". Listen, I can relate. I'm no stranger to exchanging my most important wants for something RIGHT NOW. But, one thing I can tell you is that I was always left unfulfilled, because right now wants are temporary. **When temporary things lead you to compromise, you**

dismiss yourself from the grand prize. So, I encourage you not to compromise and keep your eyes on the prize. Your future you will thank you for it. #Domin8YourDay

***

Q&A

Are you constantly exchanging what you want the most for something you want right now?

Why do you keep making this exchange?

What is the thing you want most?

Why do you want it?

What can you do to challenge yourself not to settle for temporary wants?

How will you benefit from this?

How will the people who care about you the most and the people you care about the most benefit from you not exchanging what you want most for what you want now?

15

The Greatest Attitude Is Gratitude

Find a reason to be grateful in everything that occurs in your life. As the old saying goes "It can always be worse." **The best posture that you can have is one of gratefulness.** Feel free to look at life through the lens of the cup being half-full or half-empty. Just so long as you make sure that you are grateful for your cup. So, starting today, focus on exuding GR8FUL VIBES ONLY. Your future you will thank you for it. **#Domin8YourDay**

Q&A

Name 3 things that you are grateful for?

Why are you grateful for these things?

Is gratitude something that you are intentional about expressing? Why or why Not?

What can you do to continue being intentional in your gratitude?

How will you benefit from this?

How will the people who care about you the most and the people you care about the most benefit from you being grateful as often as possible?

16

Don't Let Where You Are, Discourage You From Where You're Going

A few months ago, after teaching my empowerment session, I spoke with a young man who shared with me that he wasn't excited about where he was physically or mentally. He didn't like the fact that he was living in a transitional home and it was messing with his mind. What I quickly picked up from this young man is that he felt like this was the end of his rope. Like this was the end-all-be-all. But, I'm going to tell you like I told him. **Your current situation determines where you start not where you end up.** Instead of looking at your current situation as the finale, view it as an episode that's furthering your story. Stay strong through the episodes in your story. Your future you will thank you for it. #Domin8YourDay

* * *

Q&A

Is there something in your life that is discouraging you?

What about it is discouraging?

How will you make a perspective change?

How will you benefit from this?

How will the people who care about you the most and the people you care about the most benefit from you not allowing where you are now to discourage you from where you are going?

IF YOU GET KNOCKED DOWN, GET BACK UP

17

If You Get Knocked Down, Get Back Up

There's a huge difference between getting knocked down and getting knocked out. When you get knocked out, there is no getting up. It's over. It's done. It's a wrap. Night-night. If you've ever been knocked out, then you know what I mean. But, when you get knocked down, you don't have to stay down. You still have an opportunity to get back up. A mentor of mine once told me that if I get knocked down, try my best to land face up. Because if I could see up, then I could get up. Listen, being knocked down doesn't knock you out of the fight. **You are still capable of being the champion that you were created to be.** Two years ago, my brother Andre "S.O.G." Ward fought the fight of his life. He faced Sergey Kovalev for three light-heavyweight world title belts. In this particular fight, Dre was the challenger. In the 2nd round of his boxing match, he got knocked down, but he didn't stay down. He picked himself up. He kept fighting. He persevered and won the fight. He became the new Light-Heavyweight champion of the world. He showed the true heart of a champion. I want the same thing for you. When life punches you in the face and you get knocked down, just make sure you get your butt back up and win your fight. Your future you will thank you for it. **#Domin8YourDay**

Q&A

When is the last time you've been knocked down?

Was it a mental, physical or emotional knock down?

What was your motivation to get up?

How can you benefit from this experience?

How will the people who care about you the most and the people you care about the most benefit from you getting up after you get knocked down?

18

Stop Your Noise So You Can Move With Poise

I know you deal with a lot of noise every single day. Maybe it's people in your ear who are talking or worse, gossiping. Maybe it's social media at your fingertips. Or maybe it's just the random busyness of life. But, even with all of that going on, I want you to make time in your day to make all that noise go away. Choose to control what you let in and what you shut out. Listen, **time given to intentional thinking can lead to purposeful action.** And, I want you to be purposeful...daily. So, challenge yourself to stop your noise. Your future you will thank you for it. **#Domin8YourDay**

✳ ✳ ✳

Q&A

What type of noise do you allow in your space on

a regular basis?

What parts of that noise can you do without?

What can you do to make this noise stop?

When will you do it?

How will you benefit from this?

How will the people who care about you the most and the people you care about the most benefit from you stopping your noise so you can move with poise?

19

Celebrate Wins Daily

Celebrate every win, every single day. It doesn't matter if the win is small or big. Make time to celebrate it. Whether you're celebrating the fact that you checked off everything on your to-do list, or the fact that you smiled at someone who has been negative to you all week. Maybe you held your tongue and didn't cuss out that person who cut you off on the road. Whatever it is, celebrate it. **When you celebrate your wins you set yourself up to celebrate again.** So, keep celebrating. Your future you will thank you for it. **#Domin8YourDay**

✳ ✳ ✳

Q&A

When is the last time that you celebrated a win?

What was the win?

Why did you celebrate it?

What can you do to celebrate your next win?

How will you benefit from this?

How will the people who care about you the most and the people you care about the most benefit from you celebrating wins daily?

DEPLOY SUBTRACTION TO EVERY DISTRACTION

20

Deploy Subtraction To Every Distraction

I don't know about you but sometimes I get distracted easily. These distractions come in the form of thoughts. These thoughts aren't always negative either; sometimes the thoughts are positive. Usually about things I love or have a passion for. But, here's what I've learned: if it distracts me from my pathway to purpose then I must subtract it. My guy Wordsmith said something to me that I'm going to say to you:

"Don't let the distraction become the attraction."

Even if the distraction is something good, you must take it out of your equation. I want you to **utilize the process of subtraction to every single distraction that comes your way,** even the good ones! Remember, good is the enemy of great and we are shooting for *PhenomenAmazing*.

Don't be a victim of your distractions; subtract them! Your future you will thank you for it. **#Domin8YourDay**

*** *** ***

Q&A

What are your major distractions at the moment?

Why do you consider them distractions?

How long have you allowed yourself to be distracted?

What will you do to subtract these from your path of purpose?

How will you benefit from this?

How will the people who care about you the most and the people you care about the most benefit from you subtracting every distraction?

21

Make Time For Those Who Are For You, Not Just With You

We should always put an effort into making time for the people who have our back, no matter what. We should **frequently and openly acknowledge those who truly want to see us win and shine.** Be sure NOT to neglect the ones who are there by giving your time to those who only want to take from you. So, give your perfect effort to schedule MORE time for those that have your best interest at heart. Your future you will thank you for it. **#Domin8YourDay**

Q&A

Who are the people in your life that are for you, not just with you?

When is the last time that you made time for these people?

How does it make you feel that they are for you? Why?

Do you know people that are just with you?

What can you do to push yourself to stop giving them your time?

How will you benefit from this?

How will the people who care about you the most and the people you care about the most benefit from you making more time for those who are for you?

YOUR ACTIONS SHOWCASE YOUR VALUES

22

Your Actions Showcase Your Values

#Transpar3ntTuesday Entry

"Your actions showcase your values." I am constantly reminding myself of this. Values are a person's principles or standards of behavior. A few examples of values are power, respect, honesty, fame, popularity, religion, integrity, athletic ability, love and human life. Over the years, I've come to learn that my actions stem from my VALUES...my true values. Not what I SAY I value, but what I actually value. For example, saying that you value honesty, respect and trustworthiness means nothing if you're constantly being dishonest, disrespectful and untrustworthy. By your actions, you are proving that you truly DON'T value any of those things at all. You must go beyond saying you value something just because it sounds good. **Words mean nothing without ACTION**. If you value honesty, put forth your perfect effort to be honest. If you value respect, be sure that you are someone who respects others. It is through these actions you showcase your values. I encourage you to make sure that your ACTIONS are in alignment with the VALUES you want to showcase. Your future you will thank you for it. **#Domin8YourDay**

Q&A

What are your TOP 5 core values?

Would people know these values are what you value the most by simply observing your actions?

How will the people who care about you the most and the people you care about the most benefit from you making sure that your values are in alignment with the person that you aspire to become?

How will you benefit from making sure that your values are in alignment with the person that you aspire to become?

I'M POSSIBLE IS THE NEW IMPOSSIBLE

23

I'm Possible Is the New Impossible

I want to challenge you to take this perspective when it comes to the word impossible. That's right. You heard me. IMPOSSIBLE. I want you to take that one word and split it in two. Instead of impossible say to yourself I'M POSSIBLE. Because YOU. ARE. POSSIBLE. Listen, before the first plane took off, people said that was impossible. Before the first person stepped on the moon, they said that was impossible. Let me give you a personal experience. In 2007, I met my brother JD. And, of all places, we met in Brisbane, Australia. Yes, this kid from Richmond, California flew 15 hours to the other side of the world to go on tour. Impossible is nothing! If anyone tells you different, remember these words: **All things are possible**. You have untapped potential on the inside of you that is waiting to be unlocked. The key was given to you when you woke up this morning. So, go for it. Make the impossible possible. Your future you will thank you for it. **#Domin8YourDay**

Q&A

What are some things in your life that you've previously considered to be impossible?

Why did you feel those things were impossible?

What are some things in your future that you have already written off as impossible?

How can you see these things as possible?

How will you benefit from this?

How will the people who care about you the most and the people you care about the most benefit from you believing that you are possible?

24

Be The Person That You Needed Someone To Be For You

We sometimes rely on someone to be what we need. Whether that someone is a parent who shows more unconditional love and understanding, or maybe a coach that is more transformational than transactional. Maybe we need a friend who listens more and is empathetic to our situation. Look, while others may not always know what you need, **you know what you need and how it feels to need someone.** We cannot control if we'll always have someone "be the person" for us BUT we can control "being that person" for others. So, from this moment on, challenge yourself to be that someone for someone else. Your future you will thank you for it. **#Domin8YourDay**

* * *

Q&A

What type of person do you need someone to be for you right now?

What are their characteristics?

Why do you need someone like this?

What can you do to go forth and be that someone for someone else?

How will you benefit from this?

How will the people who care about you the most and the people you care about the most benefit from you being the person that you needed someone to be for you?

25

Give Effortlessly

Give. Give. Give! Happiness is more often found in giving than getting. I want to challenge you to be an effortless giver! **Find someone to give something to without any expectation of getting anything in return.** It could be a smile, money, a compliment, food, a handshake, a hug or a word of encouragement. My personal acronym for GIVE is Generosity Intensifies Value Exponentially. Plainly put: When you give, value grows. So, Just Give It...with no expectation. Your future you will thank you for it. **#Domin8YourDay**

Q&A

When was the last time that you gave something without expecting to get something in return?

What did you give?

Why did you give it?

How can you apply this experience to other situations moving forward?

What can you do to challenge yourself to give effortlessly?

How will you benefit from this?

How will the people who care about you the most and the people you care about the most benefit from you giving effortlessly?

ELIMINATE EXCUSES OR EXCUSES WILL ELIMINATE YOU

26

Eliminate Excuses Or Excuses Will Eliminate You

Excuses excuse you from being the person that you were created to be! Nobody cares about your sorry excuses. You don't even really care about them. Excuses are just another way of taking the easy road. But, when has the "easy" way ever lead to success? Probably, never. **It's time to eliminate excuses before they eliminate you.** That's right. Continuing to make excuses, will only keep you from being exceptional. And, I want you to be EXCEPTIONAL. So, I encourage you to start a new habit today. Make adjustments instead of making excuses. Your future you will thank you for it. **#Domin8YourDay**

* * *

Q&A

Are you making excuses for yourself?

What adjustments can you make instead of making excuses?

How will you benefit from this?

How will the people who care about you the most and the people you care about the most benefit from you eliminating excuses?

27

Show Up And Show Out

Show up and Show out! A teacher once told me that for me to be great I had to "show up". **It's not enough to just show up physically, but you must show up mentally as well.** The tragedy is that there are many of us who are not showing up at all. We all want a better life, but it's meaningless if we aren't doing anything productive to make it happen. Now, you may be showing up consistently, which is great. But, I want to challenge you to take it to the next level and SHOW OUT! Showing out is taking your great and making it *PhenomenAmazing*. And, I believe that you were created to do just that. So, do yourself and those that are counting on you a favor...show up and show out in every moment of your day. Your future you will thank you for it. **#Domin8YourDay**

Q&A

In what areas of your life do you need to show up and show out? Why?

When is the last time you showed up and showed out?

What was the situation?

How can you apply the mindset from that situation to every situation?

How will you benefit from this?

How will the people who care about you the most and the people you care about the most benefit from you showing up and showing out?

STRETCH YOURSELF SO YOU DON'T LET YOURSELF STAY STAGNANT

28

Stretch Yourself So You Don't Let Yourself Stay Stagnant

Stretch yourself!! Today is the day that you go beyond your norm. You've been doing the same thing over and over again expecting different results for a long time. THAT STOPS TODAY! **It's time to get comfortable with being uncomfortable**. But, in order to do that, you must first make yourself uncomfortable. Once you do this, you will begin to grow like never before. So, I encourage you to be committed to growth. Don't be overly concerned with getting it wrong. Your future you will thank you for it. **#Domin8YourDay**

Q&A

In what areas of your life do you need to stretch yourself and get uncomfortable? Why?

What are you going to do today to get outside of your comfort zone?

How will you benefit from this?

How will the people who care about you the most and the people you care about the most benefit from you stepping outside of your comfort zone and growing?

29

Actions Are Followed By Rewards Or Consequences...Sometimes Both

Every action has a reward or a consequence. That's right. All of your current and future actions will have a reward or consequence. Sometimes an action will even have both. Let me break that down for you with a personal experience. Recently I was in the gym with my two sons and I dunked. Yes, the thirty-six-year-old encouragement expert dunked a basketball on a regulation hoop. The reward is that my two sons saw me dunk and now I have bragging rights. The consequence is that I felt like I needed to be rushed to the hospital because of the pain I created down my right leg. I'll be the first to say that this is what happens when you think you still got it but you don't stretch (lol). Okay, stop laughing now and listen. Always remember that **there will be an outcome to your actions.** So, be very sure that you'll be okay with the rewards or consequences of those actions. Your future you will thank you for it. **#Domin8YourDay**

✳ ✳ ✳

Q&A

When was the last time you received a reward or consequence for your actions?

What was the reward?

What was the consequence?

Have you ever done something and received a reward and a consequence?

If yes, what did you do?

On a scale from 1 to 5, with 1 being <u>never</u> and 5 being <u>always</u>, how often do you think about the rewards and consequences of your actions?

How can you push yourself to consider the consequences and the rewards of your actions moving forward?

How will you benefit from this?

How will the people who care about you the most

and the people you care about the most benefit from your defining moments?

YOUR WHY IS WORTH KNOWING

30

Your Why Is Worth Knowing

To be the most effective person that you were created to be, you must know your "WHY". On the largest scale, your WHY is the very reason for you being put on this earth. It's the thing you were creatively created for. The thing you were masterfully made for. Deliberately designed for. Beautifully built for. It's the reason that you are exactly who you are. Your WHY is the reason that you do what you do, how you do it. **Knowing your WHY allows you to add massive meaning to your life.**

Listen. Once I learned my why, my life began to drastically change for the better. My focus became unwavering concentration. My hunger for helping people turned into starvation. And, my passion created *PhenomenAmazing* platforms like never before. So, let me say it again, "YOUR WHY IS WORTH KNOWING". Because once you know your why, you'll find a way for every how. Figure out your why ASAP. Your future you will thank you for it. **#Domin8YourDay**

Q&A

What is your WHY?

How will you use the statements presented to you in this book to continue KNOWING and LIVING your WHY?

How will the people who care about you the most and the people you care about the most benefit from you knowing your WHY?

How will you benefit from knowing your WHY?

REFLECTION TIME

Now that you've finished the book, I encourage you to go back over the statements that resonated with you the most and share your findings with a few trustworthy people. What are your top 5 statements that you're willing to commit your perfect effort to everyday?

1. _____

2. _____

3. _____

4. _____

5. _____

If you want to change your life, it starts with you taking action. No one is going to do it for you. So, put in the necessary work instead of being complacent. The life you've only dreamed of is waiting on the you that you need to become. Get to it! **#Domin8YourDay**

ABOUT THE AUTHOR

The Encouragement Expert, Dwight Taylor Sr., is a TED-talker and award-winning professional communicator who has been endorsed by legendary speaker Les Brown. He has been seen and heard on SHOWTIME, FOX, CBS, BET, ESPN and JUCEtv. This Bishop O'Dowd alum earned his Bachelors of Science Degree from California State University, Fresno.

Public speaking, conducting workshops, teaching empowerment sessions, coaching, consulting and music are avenues of communication that Dwight uses to encourage people to be the best version of themselves, every single day with no moments off.

Whether giving motivational presentations in Australia and the Cayman Islands or standing in a DMV line in America, encouraging greatness with empowering statements is what Dwight does on a daily basis.

He currently resides in Sacramento, CA with his wife, Kia, their 3 children, Dwight Jr., Isaiah, Haleiha and their two younger siblings, Jaysson and Mei-Mei.

CONTACT THE AUTHOR

Mail: Attn: Dwight Taylor Sr.
PO Box 464
Suisun City, CA 94585
Email : DwightTaylorSr@gmail.com
Website: www.DwightTaylorSr.com

STAY CONNECTED

1. Join Dwight's mailing list at www.dwighttaylorsr.com

2. Receive encouraging text messages from Dwight

3. Subscribe to Dwight's YouTube channel for videos that empower, encourage, entertain and educate.

4. Follow **#Domin8YourDay** to stay up-to-date on the journey

5. Follow Dwight online:

    a. Youtube.com/DwightTaylorSr

    b. Instagram & Twitter @DwightTaylorSr

    c. Facebook: Search for Dwight Taylor Sr

    d. Snapchat: DwightTaylorSr

    e. Soundcloud.com/DwightTaylorSr

    f. Itunes/Google Play/Stitcher - Search: Dwight Taylor Sr

Get connected online at
www.DwightTaylorSr.com

ACKNOWLEDGMENTS

Pops, Grans, Gam, Papa Ray, mama, dad, Paula, Lani, Deedee, Uncle Clifford, Uncle Junior, Uncle Tennyson, Lisa, Phillip, T-mac, Anne, D'artagnan, Jo'siah, Big Mike, Mike Jr., Daniel, Jordan, Ryan, Mikale, Sissy, Diamond, Lexi, Mei Mei, Young Win, Brady, G.Hill-Thomas, Hodoh, Ivory, PacMan, Denise, Pastor Smoke, Lady Jenn, Wordsmith, T.Stew, Levi, Dre, Squint and the rest of my family...I LOVE YALL!

Rhiannon White-Andrews, thanks so much for your PhenomenAmazing input and being the first teacher to use my book for the growth-mindset portion of your class. I am beyond grateful for you and all that you do. Shoutout to Principal Hollander too for giving the "thumbs up".

Jaysson, you went from being my younger brother to my right hand man! This book wouldn't be what it is without your sacrifice. Thank you. Love you JT!

Bre, my oldest younger sister, thanks for taking time to read this before anyone else. Your feedback meant more than you know. I'm looking forward to reading what you've been working on. Love you sis!

Regina Lee, thank you for making time in your busy schedule to read through this book and assist me in making some necessary adjustments. I greatly appreciate it.

Emma Barry, thank you for your effort, sacrifice, and willingness to ride along with me on this wild wild journey. Working with me is a task. You handled it with class. Beyond grateful to have you as my editor. Love Ya!

Cortney, my brother from another mother, THANK YOU... for everything. I can't even put into words how grateful I am to have you in my life and on my side. My brand wouldn't be what it is without you my man. We've been at this thing for 6+ years and you've always delivered above and beyond my expectations. Oh yea, YOU KILLED THIS BOOK COVER and every other graphic and website you've created for me over the years (way too many to count, lol). This book has you all over it! On a personal note, thank you for being that ONE. You already know what it is bro. So, in your words, "Let's make it better by going up together". Love you and appreciate you big time!

My three kids, Dwight Jr., Isaiah and Haleiha. You are my daily inspiration. You keep me accountable even when you don't know it. Because of you, I know how to love unconditionally. I love you!

And to Kia. My wife. Words can't express how grateful and thankful I am for your support and encouragement throughout this process. You've outdone yourself. You've sacrificed more than I could've imagined you would. THANK YOU! You know I can talk/write for days, but the way your love language is set up, I'll give my PERFECT EFFORT to *showing* you my appreciation. I "blue heart" YOU.